P9-BYO-309

THE PALACE OF
HOLYROODHOUSE
OFFICIAL GUIDEBOOK

THE ROYAL COLLECTION

Published by
Royal Collection Enterprises Ltd
St James's Palace
London SW1A 1JR

For a complete catalogue of current publications, please write to the address above, or visit our website on www.royal.gov.uk

© 2002 Royal Collection Enterprises Ltd
Text by Ian Gow and reproductions of all items in the Royal Collection © 2002 HM Queen Elizabeth II

117374

All rights reserved. Except as permitted under current legislation, no part of this publication may be photocopied, stored in a retrieval system, published, performed in public, adapted, broadcast, transmitted, recorded or reproduced in any form or by any means, without the prior permission of the copyright owner.

ISBN 1 902163 12 5
British Library Cataloguing in Publication Data
A catalogue record for this book is available from the British Library

Designed by Baseline Arts Ltd, Oxford
Produced by Book Production Consultants plc, Cambridge
Printed and bound by Norwich Colour Print Ltd

The unique status of the Palace of Holyroodhouse as a working palace means that paintings and works of art are sometimes moved at short notice. Pictures and works of art are also frequently lent from the Royal Collection to exhibitions all over the world. The arrangement of objects and paintings may therefore occasionally vary from that given in this guidebook.

The programme of restoration and development taking place at the Palace of Holyroodhouse may mean that the route visitors follow through the rooms differs occasionally from that given in the guidebook.

For ticket and booking information, please contact:
Superintendent's Office
Palace of Holyroodhouse
Edinburgh EH3 8DX

Tel: +44 (0)131 556 7371
24-hour information line: +44 (0)131 556 1096
Fax: +44 (0)131 557 5256

Website: www.royal.gov.uk
Email: holyroodhouse@royalcollection.org.uk

CONTENTS

LEFT: Detail of the fountain in the Forecourt of the palace, designed by the Scottish architect Robert Matheson.

FRONTISPIECE: The quadrangle of the palace, part of the rebuilding programme initiated by Charles II in 1671.

INTRODUCTION

THE QUEEN IS HEAD OF STATE of the United Kingdom of Great Britain and Northern Ireland. She is also Head of the Commonwealth. The Palace of Holyroodhouse is her official home and office in her Scottish capital, and it was here that she appointed her Scottish First Minister in May 1999. Here she also received all the new Members of the Scottish Parliament on 1 July 1999.

The monarch's direct powers these days are limited. as a constitutional sovereign The Queen normally acts on the advice of her Ministers. Nevertheless the Government, the Judiciary and the Armed Services all act in The Queen's name and the monarch is the principal symbol of national unity. She is kept closely informed about all aspects of national life and the Prime Minister has a private audience with her every week when she is in London, and once during her annual visit to Balmoral Castle, her Scottish country home, in the summer. The Scottish First Minister now also has regular audiences with The Queen. The Queen has certain residual 'prerogative' powers – particularly to appoint the Prime Minister, to grant or withhold a dissolution of Parliament and to appoint the Scottish First Minister.

As well as being Head of the Commonwealth, The Queen is Head of State of sixteen of its fifty-four member countries. She is kept informed of events throughout the Commonwealth, and is present at the two-yearly meetings of the Commonwealth Heads of Government. In 1997 this meeting was held at Holyroodhouse (see pages 8-9).

The Queen spends a week in residence at the palace every summer, during which time she carries out a wide range of official engagements throughout Scotland, often accompanied by her Scottish Ministers. The Duke of Hamilton (Hereditary Keeper of the Palace), the Royal Company of Archers (The Queen's Bodyguard in Scotland) and the High Constables of Holyroodhouse are all on duty during her stay.

THE WEST FRONT OF THE PALACE, showing James V's massive Tower of 1528–32 on the left, and the central entrance, surmounted by the Royal Arms of Scotland and the crowned cupola of 1677. The central entrance and right-hand tower can be seen in Sir David Wilkie's painting of 1822-30, *The Entrance of George IV at Holyroodhouse*, illustrated on page 20.

A garden party held at the Palace of Holyroodhouse in 1953, the year of The Queen's Coronation.

The Queen also usually holds an investiture in the Great Gallery for people in Scotland whose achievements have been recognised in the Honours Lists published every year at New Year and on The Queen's official birthday. She and The Duke of Edinburgh hold a garden party to which Scots from all walks of life are invited, and dinner parties are regularly held in the Royal Dining Room. When there is a Service of the Order of the Thistle, Scotland's ancient Order of Chivalry, at Saint Giles' Cathedral in Edinburgh, The Queen and The Duke of Edinburgh give a lunch party for the Knights and Ladies of the Order in the Throne Room. The Queen also gives audiences in the Morning Drawing Room, including one for the Lord High Commissioner to the General Assembly of the Church of Scotland.

From time to time foreign heads of state are invited for a state visit to Scotland, and on these occasions they stay with The Queen and The Duke of Edinburgh at the palace and are entertained to a state banquet in the Great Gallery. Thus Holyroodhouse is still very much a working royal residence, and a centre of national life whenever The Queen or other members of the Royal Family and Household stay.

Sir Sean Connery being knighted by The Queen at an investiture held in the Great Gallery of Holyroodhouse in July 2000.

The start of the 21st century sees Holyroodhouse poised on the brink of two exciting developments that will transform the palace. Within the Mews, the Royal Collection Trust is breathing new life into two 19th-century buildings, originally the Holyroodhouse Free Church and the Duchess of Gordon's School. These are being transformed by Benjamin Tindall Architects to create a new exhibition space that will be known as 'The Queen's Gallery, Edinburgh'. State-of-the-art environmental controls will enable this newly created exhibition space to display a very wide range of treasures from the Royal Collection, including Old Master drawings from the celebrated holdings at Windsor Castle.

At the same time, adjacent to the palace gates, the site selected for the new Scottish Parliament is also being developed. An international competition was held for the design of the new building, and was won in 1998 by the late Enric Miralles, the Spanish architect. This project will transform the whole Canongate district and will also embrace the restoration of 17th-century Queensberry House, one of the courtiers' town mansions built in close proximity to Charles II's new baroque palace, by Lord Hatton, brother to the Duke of Lauderdale, in 1681.

Artist's impression of The Queen's Gallery, Edinburgh.

TIMELINE

THIS TIMELINE SHOWS some of the most significant developments in the history of Holyroodhouse, from Augustinian monastery to royal palace, through the embellishments of James V and the drama of Mary, Queen of Scots' reign to its rebuilding under Charles II and development as the monarch's official residence in Scotland.

1651
Scottish coronation of Charles II

1305
Execution of William Wallace in London

1566
Murder of David Rizzio, Mary, Queen of Scots' Italian secretary, at the palace

1567
Murder of Lord Darnley, Mary, Queen of Scots' second husband

1528-32
James V builds Tower

1128
David I founds Augustinian monastery on the site of the Palace of Holyroodhouse

1297
English defeated at Stirling by the Scots

1314
Battle of Bannockburn Scots defeat the English

1503
James IV adds to the palace before marrying Margaret Tudor

1535-36
New west front of the palace created

1587
Execution of Mary, Queen of Scots at Fotheringhay Castle

1633
Scottish coronation of Charles I

CANMORE		BALLIOL	BRUCE	STUART						CHARLES I	COMMON
DAVID I	MARGARET (Maid of Norway)	JOHN BALLIOL	ROBERT I (The Bruce)	JAMES III	JAMES IV	JAMES V	MARY, QUEEN OF SCOTS	JAMES VI & I		CHARLES I	PROTEC
1124-1153	1286-1290	1292-1296	1306-1329	1460-1488	1488-1513	1513-1542	1542-1567	1567-1603 1603-1625		1625-1649	1649

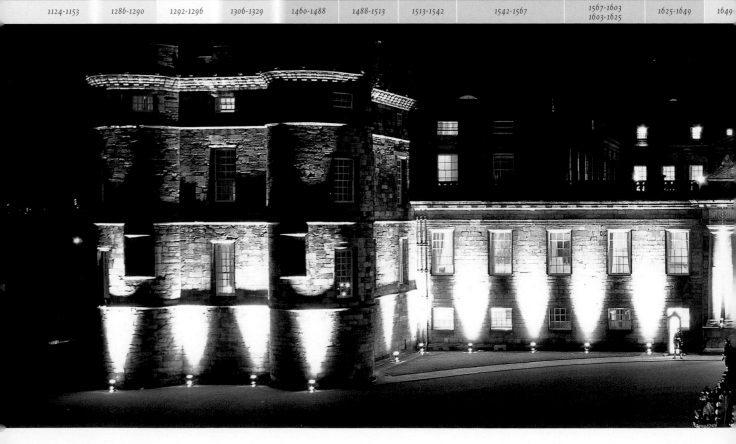

1911
State Visit of
King George V
and Queen Mary

1671
Rebuilding
work begins
at the palace

1795
Royal Apartments
offered to the
comte d'Artois
(later Charles X of
France)

1850
Queen Victoria visits
the Palace of
Holyroodhouse for
the first time

2002
Queen
Elizabeth II's
Golden Jubilee

1745
Bonnie Prince Charlie holds court
at the palace

1822
George IV's State
Visit to Scotland

1999
Scottish First
Minister
appointed by
The Queen

1707
Act of Union
between Scotland
and England —
parliaments
united

1977
Queen Elizabeth II's Silver Jubilee

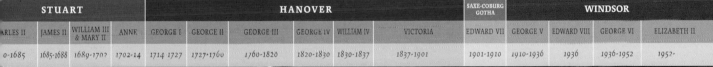

STUART				HANOVER						SAXE-COBURG GOTHA	WINDSOR			
CHARLES II	JAMES II	WILLIAM III & MARY II	ANNE	GEORGE I	GEORGE II	GEORGE III	GEORGE IV	WILLIAM IV	VICTORIA	EDWARD VII	GEORGE V	EDWARD VIII	GEORGE VI	ELIZABETH II
0-1685	1685-1688	1689-1702	1702-14	1714 1727	1727-1760	1760-1820	1820-1830	1830-1837	1837-1901	1901-1910	1910-1936	1936	1936-1952	1952-

The exterior of Holyroodhouse, floodlit for the Commonwealth Heads of Government meeting in 1997.

9

THE HISTORY OF THE PALACE

The Holy Rood

The Abbey of Holyrood probably took its name from its most precious relic, a fragment of the True Cross, which had been brought to Scotland by King David I's mother, St Margaret. In later medieval legend, the King founded his abbey on the spot where, while out hunting, he had a vision of a beautiful stag with a cross or 'rood' between its antlers. The symbol of the abbey, and its successor the palace, is therefore a stag's head with the horns framing a cross.

THE PALACE OF HOLYROODHOUSE has its origins in the Augustinian monastery founded on the site by King David I of Scotland (r. 1124–53) in 1128.

As a royal foundation the Abbey of Holyrood prospered, and at the turn of the twelfth century, devoted its wealth to an ambitious architectural programme. The legendary connection in name between King David's abbey and his vision while out hunting probably does in fact hold the clue to the development of the palace, because, as Edinburgh became recognised as Scotland's capital, her kings preferred to establish their quarters in the Abbey of Holyrood, surrounded by its hunting park, rather than in Edinburgh Castle, exposed to the elements on its rock. The abbey thus became the setting for many events in Scotland's history.

By degrees, however, the palace buildings came to eclipse in size and importance those of the abbey. James IV (r.1488–1513) certainly made additions to them in anticipation of his marriage to Margaret Tudor, daughter of Henry VII, which was celebrated in the abbey in 1503, but nothing survives of these works except the fragmentary trace of his gatehouse, sadly demolished in 1753. His successor, James V (r. 1513–42), left a much more substantial monument in his massive Tower, constructed between 1528 and 1532. Its progress can be followed in the surviving *Accounts of the Masters of Works* (now in the Scottish Record Office) and it supplies the matrix for the modern palace.

Between 1535 and 1536, James V embarked on a second ambitious building campaign to create a new west front for the palace, south of the Royal Apartment

James V, King of Scotland, and Mary of Guise in a double portrait from Falkland Palace.

in his Tower. With its great expanses of glazing and ornamental crestings, this new addition was domestic rather than defensive and may have been begun in anticipation of the King's marriage on 1 January 1537 to Madeleine Valois, daughter of Francis I, King of France.

Madeleine died only forty days after arriving in Scotland, but French influence was preserved through James V's second marriage in 1538 to Mary of Guise, who was crowned in the abbey.

When James V died in 1542 his daughter, Mary, Queen of Scots, was only a few days old. Sent to France as a child she married the heir to the French throne in 1558. In July 1559 Mary became Queen of France when her husband succeeded to the throne as Francis II, but he died in 1560. The young Catholic Queen then returned as a widow to what had now become a strongly Protestant Scotland.

Many of the dramatic events of Mary's short reign as Queen of Scots took place in the abbey and palace of Holyroodhouse. These included her marriage to Henry Stuart, Lord Darnley; Darnley's murder of her secretary, David Rizzio; and following Darnley's own mysterious death, her subsequent marriage to James Hepburn, 4th Earl of Bothwell. No Scottish monarch was to be more closely associated with Holyroodhouse than Mary, Queen of Scots, and the palace subsequently became a shrine to her cult.

Early 18th-century engraving showing James IV's gatehouse of 1503.

One of the heraldic supporters of the Royal Arms of James V of Scotland (1513–42), in the wall by the palace entrance in Abbey Strand.

The palace as depicted in the so-called English Spy Map of c.1544.

Paul van Somer, *James VI and I*, 1618

Sir Peter Lely, *Charles II*, c.1665–70

THE FOUNDATION INSCRIPTION in the quadrangle for Charles II's rebuilding of the palace. In abbreviated form it reads 'founded by Robert Mylne, Master Mason, July 1671'.

Although Mary, Queen of Scots' son, James VI of Scotland (r. 1567–1625), held his councils here, his succession to the English throne in 1603 could not but lead to a dimming of the palace's glories. It had to be renovated for his return in 1617 and again in 1633 for the Scottish coronation of his son, Charles I (r. 1625–49). Charles I's religious intransigence upset both his Scottish and his English subjects, and led to the signing of the National Covenant in Scotland and the Civil War in England. In the strife which followed the execution of Charles I in 1649 and the coronation of his son Charles II in Scotland in 1651, the palace was damaged by Oliver Cromwell's troops and very poorly repaired.

THE REBUILDING OF THE PALACE

Charles II (r. 1660–85) never returned to Scotland after his restoration to the English throne, but he took pains to have the palace of his Stuart ancestors repaired after the ravages of Cromwell's troops.

Building work began in 1671. The King took a personal interest in the practical details of the plan but he also had a reliable team on the site. The work was effectively directed by his Secretary of State for Scotland, James Maitland, 1st Duke of Lauderdale (1616–82), who had a passion for building and luxurious and fashionable tastes in interior decoration, as can still be seen in his houses at Ham, near Richmond in Surrey, and at Thirlestane Castle near Lauder in Scotland. The King's Surveyor of Royal Works was Sir William Bruce, who was known as a skilled architect, while Robert Mylne, the King's Master Mason, who came from a dynasty of craftsmen, was responsible for the actual execution of the building work. The combined talents of these three men ensured that Holyroodhouse emerged as the key monument in the history of Scottish classical architecture. Bruce's design employed the three orders of architecture – Doric, Ionic and Corinthian – with a grammatical correctness that was new to Scotland, while the sumptuous interiors overseen by Lauderdale, with their fine plasterwork, carving and decorative painting, blending into a superb baroque unity, were admired and emulated with varying degrees of success in many of Scotland's castles and country houses.

The grandiose initial scheme was in fact curtailed after scrutiny by the King, who insisted on practicality. Charles II required only a single new Royal Apartment to the east, overlooking the proposed new Privy Garden, while the old Royal Apartment in James V's Tower was patched up and subsequently assigned to his Queen, Catherine of Braganza. A new chapel was cancelled in favour of making the Abbey Church the Chapel Royal. The second floor of the palace was to provide accommodation for the Court during the King's residence, while in his absence it would provide accommodation for the officers of state (in a spirit of enlightened self-interest Lauderdale, who was among these officers,

THE REBUILDING OF THE PALACE

Thomas Flatman, *James Maitland,*
1st Duke of Lauderdale, early 1670s

typically ensured that the decoration of the upper floor was almost as splendid as that of the State Apartment below).

The success of Bruce's design was the result of continuity with the earlier buildings – a deliberate element in the programme for the rebuilding. James V's Tower established the height of the new ranges around the principal courtyard, and was duplicated across the west front for symmetry. The early work on the west front was repaired, perhaps out of piety to the King's ancestors, and the new rooms were arranged around a courtyard which was articulated by superimposed Doric, Ionic and Corinthian pilasters. The open, cloister like quadrangle on the ground floor perhaps recalled the palace's monastic origins.

THE QUADRANGLE OF THE PALACE is perhaps the clearest example for the visitor of the Doric, Ionic and Corinthian orders of architecture. Named after styles of architecture found in the buildings of Ancient Greece, the orders ascend in elaboration and visual effect. Thus the Doric order, the plainest and simplest, is seen here on the ground floor, the Ionic, with its slightly more elaborate scrolled capitals to the pilasters between the windows, is used on the first floor, while the Corinthian order, the most decorative and splendid of all, is used for the second floor.

The Royal Arms of Scotland on the west front of the palace.

The building work at Holyroodhouse is very well documented as both the account books and the tradesmens' individual vouchers have been preserved. Work proceeded rapidly so that by 1674 the King's Bedchamber and Ante-Room were 'far advanced' including their plaster ceilings of 'fyne fretwork'. By 1676, and perhaps as a result of the impact of the new work's clean-cut classicism, it was resolved to take down the old west front, including the extra storey which had been added by Cromwell, and rebuild it.

It was rebuilt in flat-faced, even-jointed (or ashlar) masonry, with a Doric frontispiece framing the Royal Arms of Scotland and surmounted by a broken pediment and a crowned cupola. At the same time, James V's original fortress-like Tower was tamed into domesticity by the removal of the iron grilles protecting its windows, and the windows themselves were sashed. The result was a satisfying blend of old and new.

The quality of the interior was the result of Lauderdale's ability to lure north a team of craftsmen who were to introduce Scotland to a new style of interior decoration. The glory of the palace is the range of virtuoso high-relief ceilings by the English plasterers John Houlbert and George Dunsterfield, who also worked for both Lauderdale and Bruce in their private houses. The Dutchman Alexander Eizat panelled the rooms in a style which blended plain classical forms with the richer decoration typical of French interiors of this date. Two more Dutchmen, Jan van Santvoort and Jacob de Wet the Younger were responsible for the vigorous sculptural enrichments and decorative painting of the interiors. Their contributions created a striking baroque unity in the few rooms that were to be completely realised, such as the King's Bedchamber.

Finally, at the end of Charles II's reign, De Wet was commissioned to create a sequence of portraits of the King and his 109 predecessors for the Great Gallery. Although the repetitive quality of De Wet's paintings has been criticised, this was a serious attempt to preserve the likenesses of the more recent Stuarts and to re-assert the Stuart right to the throne.

THE PALACE UNDER JAMES II AND VII

The new palace was to provide a suitably private residence in 1679 for the King's brother James, Duke of York, whose adherence to the Catholic religion was to lead him into difficulties when he succeeded to the throne as James II of England and VII of Scotland in 1685. He commanded that the Abbey Church be fitted up for Catholic ritual and also for the ceremonies of the Order of the Thistle. Until this could be realised, the Council Chamber, in the new south-west tower, was to be fitted up to serve as a temporary Chapel Royal. Altar plate was commissioned in London and sent north, and a Jesuit college was established in the palace precincts.

Susan Penelope Rosse, *James II and VII*, 1685

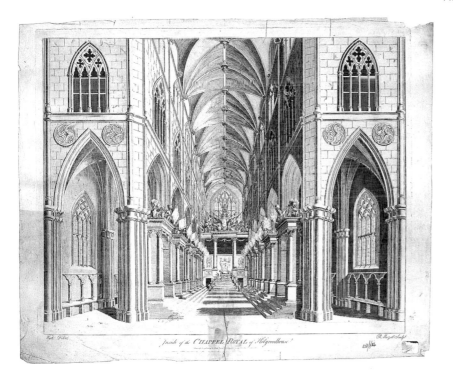

Inside of the CHAPPEL ROYAL of Holyroodhouse

Engraving of James II's Chapel Royal at Holyroodhouse, published in 1845. The classical stalls designed by William Bruce for the Knights of the Thistle are shown encasing the much earlier Gothic piers of the abbey.

However, before the Chapel Royal could be finished, William of Orange, the Dutch Protestant claimant to the throne, had landed in Devon. When this news reached Edinburgh, a riotous mob marched on the palace and destroyed every vestige of Catholicism. David Burnet, one of the priests of the Chapel Royal, had the presence of mind to rescue the most portable elements of the new altar plate and spirit them away to the north-east of Scotland, where they were preserved in the secret Catholic chapel of a farmhouse in Banffshire.

If, thereafter, the palace lacked the animation of a court, it was far from forlorn and certainly not empty. Until the Union of the Parliaments of England and Scotland in 1707, the great officers of state were given apartments on the palace's lofty second floor. There they indulged their love of display to the full, installing sumptuous furnishings and State Beds in their grace-and-favour quarters. After the Union much of this splendid furniture was re-directed to Scotland's castles and country houses. The Duke of Hamilton, who had been created Hereditary Keeper of the Palace by Charles I, appropriated the Queen's own apartments in James V's Tower, where he and his wife installed themselves in great luxury.

THE EIGHTEENTH CENTURY

The Act of Union of 1707, uniting the kingdoms of Scotland and England, dissolved the Scottish Parliament and removed the seat of Scottish power from Edinburgh (Scots MPs thenceforth met in Westminster with their English counterparts).

After the departure of the Scottish Parliament, there was to be only a brief flicker of court life at the palace, when the Young Pretender, Bonnie Prince Charlie, held court there in 1745, only to be swiftly succeeded by his victorious opponent, the Duke of Cumberland.

Louis-Gabriel Blanchet, *Prince Charles Edward Stuart, the Young Pretender (Bonnie Prince Charlie)*, 1739

BONNIE PRINCE CHARLIE

John Pettie, *Bonnie Prince Charlie*, 1892.
This painting, which was acquired by King Edward VII,
is in no way a portrait of the Prince; but it does
suggest the sense of romance and tragedy that has for
so long been a part of his history.

CHARLES EDWARD STUART, 'Bonnie Prince Charlie', was born in 1720, the grandson of the exiled James II of England and VII of Scotland (d. 1701). James II, a staunch Catholic, had been deposed from the English throne because of his faith in 1688, but both he and his son, the so-called James III, the 'Old Pretender', had vigorously maintained their claim to the throne from exile, first in France and then in Rome. The handsome, charismatic Prince, the 'Young Pretender', believed as fervently as either his father or grandfather had done in his hereditary right to rule, regarding the Hanoverian kings then on the throne of England as usurpers.

In July 1745, with the assistance of France, with whom Britain at that time was at war, Charles Edward Stuart launched an attempt to regain the crown for his father. Sailing from the French port of Nantes he landed in the western Highlands, and was immediately greeted with popular acclaim and a spontaneous rising of men from the Jacobite clans to support his cause. Bonnie Prince Charlie's 'army', as it rapidly became, first seized Perth, and at dawn on 17 September 1745, entered Edinburgh. Despite the fact that an opposing force remained in place in the Castle, the Prince and his escort entered Holyroodhouse via the Park, to the jubilation of an immense crowd gathered in the Forecourt – a scene recreated by Sir Walter Scott in his novel *Waverley*.

An English army under Sir John Cope had also landed at Dunbar on 17 September, but when it met with the Jacobite force four days later at Prestonpans the result was a resounding, and for the English, shocking defeat. Bonnie Prince Charlie returned to Edinburgh in triumph and for the next five weeks maintained a royal court at the palace, complete with balls and supper parties in the Great Gallery. At the same time, his troops laid siege to Edinburgh Castle, determined to use the gold reputed to be in its coffers to launch a full-scale invasion of England.

In London, the strength of support the Prince had generated had been met with disbelief. An English naval squadron was sent to blockade the Scottish coast, while reports of an imminent invasion by the French king Louis XV added to the general sense of panic. Although they had not seized Edinburgh Castle, the march of the rebels southward reached Derby before, short of supplies, they were forced to turn about and return to Scotland.

In the meantime, the soldiers who had been besieged in Edinburgh Castle took the opportunity to ransack the rooms (the Duke of Hamilton's apartments) that the Prince had used at Holyroodhouse. They were soon succeeded in the same rooms by William, Duke of Cumberland, youngest son of King George II, at the head of an English army, who took them over as his quarters and slept in the same State Bed so recently vacated by the Prince (illustrated on page 51).

The two armies met at Culloden on 16 April 1746. The Scots were poorly supplied, largely unpaid, and outnumbered by almost two to one. Their defeat, and the conduct of the English troops thereafter, which earned the Duke the nickname 'Butcher Cumberland', resulted in the flight of Bonnie Prince Charlie back into exile, together with many of the heads of the old Scottish clans.

The collapse of the roof of the Abbey Church in 1768, after ineffectual repairs in 1758, left the Chapel Royal in ruins. The failure to rebuild the abbey, which had been the scene of so many important events in Scottish history, was symbolic of a loss of national confidence. Similarly, the long line of portraits of the Stuart kings in the Great Gallery, which had been slashed by the sabres of English troops quartered at the palace in 1745, remained on display in this condition for many years.

This very air of neglect, however, was to foster the development of the palace as the prime Scottish tourist attraction when, during the Romantic period, the fascination with Mary, Queen of Scots' doomed reign began to cast its spell. As early as 1760 Elizabeth, Baroness Percy (later the Duchess of Northumberland) visited the palace and recorded in her diary:

> I went also to see Mary Queen of Scots' Bedchamber (a very small one it is) from
> whence David Rizzio was drag'd out and stab'd in the ante room where is some
> of his Blood which they can't get wash'd out.

The attention of visitors had begun to shift from Charles II's baroque palace, which was now deemed merely old fashioned, to the earliest part of the palace – the Royal Apartments in James V's Tower. Leading tours of visitors around Mary, Queen of Scots' rooms quickly became a profitable perquisite of the Duke of Hamilton's servants. As they were tipped for their services, these impromptu tour guides quickly became adept at dramatising every chilling detail of the story of Rizzio's brutal murder (the

The Chapel Royal in 1750, before the collapse of its roof in 1768.

17

historical facts surrounding these events are given on pages 54-56). Their storyline, thus tried and tested against tourists' reactions, was soon as ineradicable as the famous 'bloodstains' on the floor where Rizzio died. By popular belief, Mary, Queen of Scots' rooms had been preserved exactly as they were on the night of the murder, 9 March 1566, and as successive Dukes of Hamilton made improvements to their rooms on the first floor below, their old-fashioned baroque furnishings were relegated to the chambers on the second floor, and recycled as Mary, Queen of Scots' own possessions. An old State Bed was described as 'the couch of the Rose of Scotland' and was being shown to visitors together with Mary's workbox. The tapestries in the room were meanwhile described as the handiwork of French nuns. Visitors were only too willing to be deceived, as the rooms' air of neglect and decay gave them a sense of having stepped back in time, perfectly in keeping with the sensibilities of the period. The rooms' shabbiness, which the Duke's housekeeper was careful to promote, is recorded in many early views of what was regarded as 'perhaps the most interesting suite of rooms in Europe'.

An early 20th-century photograph of the Outer Chamber of Mary, Queen of Scots. This perhaps still gives something of the atmosphere of the room as it greeted earlier visitors. The brass plaque on the floor beside the open door, which is just visible in the photograph, marks the spot where Rizzio is said to have breathed his last. It is now mounted on the wall to the left.

Sir Thomas Lawrence, *Charles X*, 1825

A French Prince at Holyroodhouse

In 1795 the Royal Apartment at Holyroodhouse was offered to the comte d'Artois, brother of Louis XVI of France, who was in exile with his sons and other members of his family following the French Revolution of 1789. A compelling attraction for the Prince was the sanctuary it traditionally offered to debtors, provided they remained within the abbey precincts on weekdays. The Prince had been a leading figure at the most elegant court in Europe, but now in straitened circumstances had to accustom himself, until his return to France in 1815, to the faded splendours of Charles II's suite. This was fitted up for him by Edinburgh's leading furniture makers, Young, Trotter and Hamilton, and the handsome Edinburgh New Town furniture they supplied in 1796 stood the test of time so well that not only was it re-issued to the unfortunate Prince when he returned to Edinburgh in 1830, following the July Revolution, as the deposed King Charles X of France, but has continued in use as the primary furnishing stock of the palace down to the present day.

Sir David Wilkie, *George IV*, 1829

KING GEORGE IV'S STATE VISIT TO SCOTLAND

In 1822 George IV made a State Visit to Scotland under the stage-management of Sir Walter Scott (then at the height of his fame as a writer), and was pleasantly surprised by the warmth of his reception. The dilapidated palace was not deemed a suitable residence for a monarch with such luxurious tastes, and the King was therefore lodged amid the modern comforts of the Duke of Buccleuch's seat at Dalkeith Palace. Holyroodhouse was, however, spruced up to serve as a setting for the King's Drawing Rooms and Levees, social occasions where the King donned Highland dress in honour of his Scottish subjects.

George IV's visit placed a spotlight on the palace. In the short term the number of visitors swelled – the novelist Susan Ferrier wrote

> *I went with the Fletchers to see Holyrood, and we thought black, burning shame of ourselves for having been such gowks, as to go and look at bare rooms and an old empty throne.*

– and in the longer term, money was at last voted to be used for repairs and improvements. The King's Architect in Scotland, Sir Robert Reid, took the drastic decision to clear away the historical sprawl of buildings that clung to William Bruce's palace, leaving it foursquare and sheathed in its envelope of polished ashlar. There was, however, an important exception to this campaign of ruthless sprucing-up. On Monday 26 August 1822, the King paid a private visit to his palace 'for the purpose of inspecting its apartments', and on his departure, having been conducted by the Duke

Sir David Wilkie, *The Entrance of George IV at Holyroodhouse*, 1822-30

of Hamilton's housekeeper through Mary, Queen of Scots' apartments, 'it was the special order of his Majesty, before leaving for London, that in repairing the palace, these apartments should be preserved, sacred from every alteration.'

An important consequence of these repairs was the decision by William IV in 1834 to permit his Commissioner to the General Assembly of the Church of Scotland to take up residence in the palace during the annual meeting of the General Assembly. (A further proposal to rebuild the Chapel Royal for the Assembly in Gothic Revival mode, presented by the architect James Gillespie Graham, but actually designed by his collaborator, A. W. N. Pugin, remained on paper.)

QUEEN VICTORIA'S RETURN TO HOLYROODHOUSE

In 1842, following her coronation, Queen Victoria made her first State Visit to Scotland. The arrangements that had prevailed for George IV were repeated, and Victoria too resided at Dalkeith Palace – in fact a last-minute outbreak of scarlet fever prevented her visiting Holyroodhouse at all. However, the Queen's delight in Scotland was to have a profound effect on the royal family's life, and culminated in 1848 with the acquisition of Balmoral Castle in Aberdeenshire as Queen Victoria's Highland holiday home.

The Palace of Holyroodhouse was identified as a strategically-placed stop on the long journey north to Balmoral. For the Scots, the Queen's return in 1850 to the palace of her Stuart ancestors was seen as an event of deep emotional significance, and by degrees Holyroodhouse was reinstated as Scotland's premier royal

Sir George Hayter, *Queen Victoria in Coronation Robes*, 1838. A copy of this portrait can be seen in the Royal Dining Room (see page 29).

Franz Xaver Winterhalter, *Prince Albert*, 1859

residence. Its years of neglect did not mean that the palace was empty (the grace-and-favour tenants included Queen Victoria's own Lord Chamberlain, the Marquess of Breadalbane) so for some time the royal family had to use Charles II's apartment, which was itself beginning to acquire an antiquarian charm. Renovations were supervised from London, but the Office of Works' Scottish architect, Robert Matheson, was to develop a deep affection for the palace, and was determined to champion its cause in the face of the Treasury's cheese-paring economy. He stretched what little funds he had by appealing to the goodwill of the tradesmen of Edinburgh, who took London's financial stringency as a national slight against the Scots. Trotter's firm stripped Charles II's oak panelling of a later disfiguring coat of white paint and D. R. Hay, Scotland's leading interior decorator, cleaned the spectacular plaster ceilings and repainted them in rich colours. The pool of grace-and-favour tenants' furniture, combined with that supplied for the French princes, was supplemented with finer feathers from Buckingham Palace and a number of continental exhibition pieces. In 1856 money was found to provide the Throne Room with an antiquarian heraldic ceiling, but it was typical of the pressure on space that this important room then had to double as the Queen's Dining Room.

Matheson's real problems lay outside the palace. The once aristocratic lodgings of the Canongate had been transformed into slums. Fashionable Edinburgh had moved to the New Town, and the palace was left, jostled by the breweries and gas-works of 'Auld Reekie'. Matheson did much to improve its immediate surroundings, with Queen Victoria's husband, Prince Albert, taking a particular interest in these schemes. A new carriage approach was made to the north, avoiding the unsalubrious Canongate, but Matheson's most visible memorial is the fountain in the Forecourt of Holyroodhouse, which he modelled on an ancient example at Linlithgow Palace outside Edinburgh (a detail is illustrated on pages 2-3).

Ever since the Queen's visit in 1842 the Lord Provost of Edinburgh had been lobbying for greater public access to the palace, along the lines of that granted at Hampton Court Palace near London, which had been open to the public since 1838. In 1852 Matheson engineered an agreement with Alexander, 10th Duke of Hamilton, whereby his rooms in James V's Tower were released in exchange for a new suite above the Great Gallery. With the assistance of the Duke, the Office of Works appointed staff to show what became known as the 'Historical Apartments' on a more regular basis.

On payment of sixpence (Saturdays were free) visitors were permitted to see the Picture Gallery, Mary, Queen of Scots' Chambers and the first-floor Tower rooms, which became known as the 'Darnley Rooms'. To replace the Duke's paper hangings Matheson was able to purchase in 1864 a set of Mortlake tapestries and an entire

From Queen Victoria's *Journal*
THE QUEEN'S VISIT TO HOLYROODHOUSE

1850, Holyrood August 29:

... In the court of Holyrood was a Guard of Honour of the 93rd Highlanders, who are on duty here, & Ld. Morton, as Capt: Gen: of the Royal Archers. Mr. C. Murray received me at the door, in the name of his uncle the Duke of Hamilton, who is Keeper of the Palace. Had now safely arrived at the interesting & ancient Palace of my ancestors. Went up to our rooms, which are very handsome & comfortable. The Throne Room, Drawing room, & fine large sitting room, are all together. We wandered out with the 2 girls & Miss Hildyard, to look at the old ruined Chapel, which adjoins the Palace, & I can see from my window. It is very beautiful inside. One of the aisles is still roofed in, but the rest

is not. It was originally an Abbey, & many of the old tombstones, are those of former Friars. Afterwards it became the Chapel Royal, & Queen Mary, my unfortunate ancestress, was married to Ld. Darnley at the very altar, of which one sees the remains. The Chapel was restored in the time of James VII of Scotland & 2nd of England. Later on, it was used as a Parish Church. It contains many interesting tombs, some, of the Sutherland & Erroll families, Ld. Strathmore, – & I discovered the grave of Flora McDonald's mother. When we returned we went to look at the rooms in which Queen Mary had lived, her bedroom, – the dressingroom, into which the

murderers, who killed Rizzio, had entered, & the spot where he fell, where, as the old Housekeeper said to me 'that if the lady would stand on this side, she would see that the boards were discoloured with the blood'. Every step is full of historical recollections. Our living here, is quite an epoch in the annals of this old pile, which has seen so many deeds more bad, I fear, than good. The long Gallery, in which the Scotch Peers are elected for the Hse. of Lords, contains a collection of most frightful portraits of Kings of Scotland, beginning with a full length one of a King 330 years before Christ! The old Housekeeper did not know who I was, & Charles Murray only told her afterwards.

collection of furniture from R. G. Ellis, an Edinburgh lawyer and antiquarian. This collection was installed in the Darnley Rooms, in an attempt to match the antiquarian mood of Mary, Queen of Scots' Chambers above. Other antiquarian oddments were also purchased from time to time.

The Office of Works still had to grapple with two problems. The first was that in spite of George IV's injunction to preserve Mary, Queen of Scots' Chambers as 'sacred', an instruction later repeated by Queen Victoria, the sheer pressure of visitors required repairs to the floorboards and disintegrating textiles. Little by little, the air of exaggerated decay on which the visual appeal of the rooms depended was being lost. Secondly, as the knowledge of furniture history grew, it became glaringly obvious to more sophisticated visitors that the furniture in these rooms could not possibly be earlier than the late seventeenth century. The well-oiled patter of the guides was sometimes rudely interrupted.

THE TWENTIETH CENTURY TO THE PRESENT DAY
Although Queen Victoria's return to Holyroodhouse had transformed its fortunes, at the beginning of the twentieth century the palace still suffered from its classification as a mere 'temporary residence'. The failure to invest in more than running repairs

King George V and Queen Mary in Coronation Robes, 22 June 1911.

The Queen with 1st Battalion The Highlanders at the Palace of Holyroodhouse in 2001.

meant that its drains were deemed to be in no fit state to receive King Edward VII, who was therefore also lodged at Dalkeith Palace during his State Visit of 1903.

Edwardian enthusiasm for period furniture styles did however mean that the time had finally come for the restoration and re-arrangement of Mary, Queen of Scots' Chambers. The 'Darnley' bed and some of the chairs were sent off to the Royal School of Needlework, and the tables restored by Whytock and Reid, the Edinburgh furniture makers. Although seen as 'improvements', these measures destroyed the atmosphere that had made the rooms so visually seductive. The decision to fill the blank panels on the exterior of James V's Tower with new armorial carvings was part of the same campaign.

Later in the same decade, Holyroodhouse was selected as the site of the Scottish National Memorial to King Edward VII, following the King's death in 1910. A statue of King Edward VII by H. S. Gamley now stands against a curved screen wall, or exedra, designed by the architect George Washington Browne, facing the west front of the abbey. The Forecourt of the palace was enclosed with slender gate-piers bearing the lion and the unicorn, and with richly detailed gates and screens created under the supervision of J. Starkie Gardner, a leading authority on the craft of metal-working.

The task of adapting Holyroodhouse to the needs of the twentieth century fell to King George V and Queen Mary. Before their State Visit in 1911, a number

of changes were made. However there was still so little accommodation for the Court that temporary buildings had to be erected in the grounds of the palace. By degrees, surrounding buildings were adapted for staff use, and under the supervision of the King's Scottish architects in the Office of Works, the essential modern services, including bathrooms, electric light and lifts, were introduced into the palace with such tact that they did not intrude on its earlier fabric.

The cost of these repairs led to a review of the palace's role and it was recognised that Holyroodhouse now had equal status with the royal family's southern residences. The new appreciation of the palace's important place in the history of Scottish classical architecture was reflected in the decision to extend the public tour to embrace Charles II's State Rooms as well as Mary, Queen of Scots' historical apartments.

In the twentieth century the role of the palace continued to expand. As the official residence of The Queen in Scotland, the Palace of Holyroodhouse is today the focus of important state events, as well as less formal visits by members of the Royal Family. Its position at the end of the Royal Mile, beside the new Scottish Parliament building, reflects the part it has played in Scotland's political history. The Palace also houses a significant part of the Royal Collection, with paintings and works of art on display both within the palace itself and (from late 2002) in The Queen's Gallery.

The Queen greets Nelson Mandela at the Commonwealth Summit held at Holyroodhouse in 1997.

The Prince of Wales and two members of the Royal Company of Archers, The Queen's Bodyguard in Scotland.

MAP OF THE PALACE

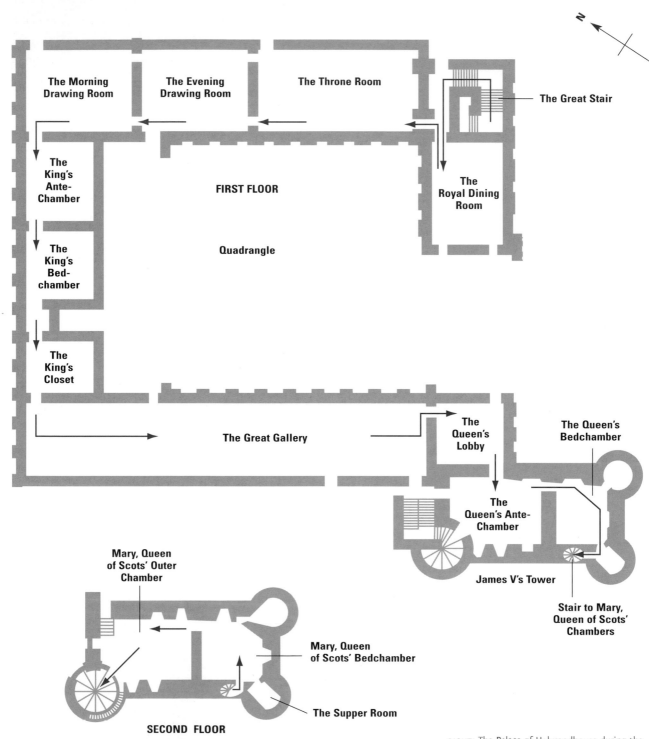

The Morning Drawing Room

The Evening Drawing Room

The Throne Room

The Great Stair

The King's Ante-Chamber

FIRST FLOOR

The Royal Dining Room

The King's Bed-chamber

Quadrangle

The King's Closet

The Great Gallery

The Queen's Lobby

The Queen's Bedchamber

The Queen's Ante-Chamber

James V's Tower

Stair to Mary, Queen of Scots' Chambers

Mary, Queen of Scots' Outer Chamber

Mary, Queen of Scots' Bedchamber

The Supper Room

SECOND FLOOR

RIGHT: The Palace of Holyroodhouse during the State Visit of the King of Norway in 1994. Matheson's fountain can be seen in the centre of the Forecourt.

THE FORECOURT AND ENTRANCE FRONT

THE FORECOURT, A PARADE GROUND
FOR FORMAL PRESENTATIONS,
CONTAINS MATHESON'S FOUNTAIN,
MODELLED ON THAT AT LINLITHGOW
PALACE

THE ROYAL ARMS OF SCOTLAND ARE
VISIBLE ABOVE THE CENTRAL
DOORWAY

TO THE LEFT OF THE FORECOURT IS
THE SCOTTISH NATIONAL MEMORIAL
TO KING EDWARD VII

THE FIRST PART OF THE PALACE seen by the visitor is the Forecourt and the entrance front. Its present ambience reflects the various nineteenth- and twentieth-century campaigns to improve the outside appearance of the palace.

Although the entrance front of the palace appears to be a uniformly symmetrical composition, the much greater antiquity of James V's Tower on the left, with its battered stonework and the scars where the iron grilles were removed from its windows, is readily apparent. By contrast, William Bruce's balancing right-hand tower of 1671 has the regularity of a toy fort. The foundations of the central connecting block incorporate James V's western extensions to his Tower of 1534–5; but the early work was taken down in 1676 when the decision was made to re-build the front in a classical style. The central doorway of the palace was conceived as a triumphal gateway, framed by Doric columns and surmounted by the Royal Arms of Scotland, carved to a design provided by Jacob de Wet in 1677. This is surmounted by a crowned cupola rising behind the broken pediment. Because the west front is so much lower than the flanking towers, the symmetrical facades of the inner court are also visible. These facades contrast strikingly with James V's massive fortified Tower.

Visitors are received in the newly restored and adapted Guardhouse, designed by Robert Matheson in a baronial style and completed in 1861. To the right of the Guardhouse gateway, a richly detailed but now very weatherworn doorway, topped by a prickly thistle, has been reset in the wall. This was salvaged from the stone walls of the old Privy Garden, demolished in 1856 when a new carriage approach to the palace was made. The scrolled ironwork of the railings on either side of the entrance front dates from the same architectural campaign. In 1920 a greater sense of enclosure of the Forecourt was at last achieved as part of the development of the site for the Scottish National Memorial to King Edward VII.

THE GREAT STAIR

THE GREAT STAIR CONTAINS THE
FIRST EXAMPLE FOR THE VISITOR OF
ONE OF THE PALACE'S EXCEPTIONAL
PLASTERWORK CEILINGS

THE FRESCO PANELS WERE
ORIGINALLY PAINTED FOR THE
PALAZZO PEDROCCA IN BRESCIA

AN ENTRANCE OFF THE CENTRAL QUADRANGLE of the palace leads directly to the Great Stair. If the exterior façades of William Bruce's courtyard are distinguished by their chaste classicism, the interior is all baroque. In the Scottish palace of the restored Stuart dynasty, architecture was used to impress and to awe. The partially cantilevered broad stone flights of the Great Stair were at the time at the cutting-edge of building technology, while the massive stone balusters add to the grandeur of this first stage on the processional route to the King's Apartments. High above there is also the first example of one of the spectacular ceilings by the virtuoso English plasterers John Houlbert and George Dunsterfield.

The three doorcases at the top of the stair were remodelled around 1800. That straight ahead leads, down an impressive enfilade of doorways, to the Morning Drawing Room.

THE CEILING ABOVE THE GREAT STAIR.
Its central compartment is surrounded by tiers of hand-modelled flowers and swags, built up on wires to give an extraordinary three-dimensional effect. (Sadly the central circular compartment never received its illusionistic decorative painting.) The life-sized figures of angels in the corners burst from their frames to brandish the symbols of kingship. The detached frescoes by the northern Italian painter Lattanzio Gambara were purchased by Prince Albert in 1856 to promote interest in the revival of fresco painting in Britain. This was a project spearheaded by Prince Albert in the context of the rebuilding of the Houses of Parliament. The examples here date from c.1550. They were transferred onto canvas, and moved from London to Holyroodhouse in 1881.

THE ROYAL DINING ROOM

ROOM PLAN →

THE ROYAL DINING ROOM WAS
ORIGINALLY THE FIRST IN THE QUEEN'S
SUITE OF ROOMS IN CHARLES II'S
PALACE

IT BECAME THE ROYAL DINING ROOM
AT THE END OF QUEEN VICTORIA'S
REIGN

AS THE OUTERMOST ROOM OF THE QUEEN'S SUITE, the Guardroom, now the
Royal Dining Room, would have been plainly finished in keeping with its
function. There was thus no earlier decorative scheme to prevent it being
transformed c.1800 by its grace-and-favour tenant into an elegant neo classical
reception room in the style of the Scottish architect Robert Adam. Sadly the
scheme is undocumented, but the plasterer was perhaps inspired by a spirit of
rivalry with the virtuoso quality of the surrounding seventeenth-century
plasterwork to produce work of equal refinement. Before it became the Royal
Dining Room, this room had been part of the Duke of Hamilton's suite. Thomas
Hall, the Edinburgh decorators, claimed credit for decorating this room in an
advertising brochure of c.1900, but there may well have been further changes under
King George V in 1910.

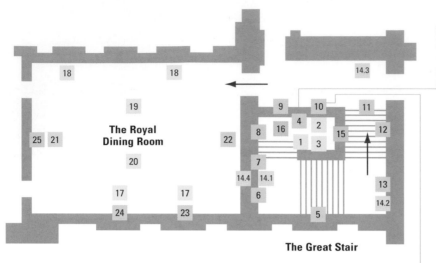

Stanley Cursiter, *The Queen Receiving the Honours of Scotland*, 1954

Lattanzio Gambara: *Neptune and Caenis, c.1550*

THE GREAT STAIR

▨ FURNITURE

1 Pair of giltwood pier tables by Whytock and Reid, made for two 18th-century alabaster table tops formerly in the collection of Pope Pius VI. Presented to King George V in 1917.

2 Set of carved oak side chairs, late 17th-century style.

3 Late 18th-century sedan chair, reputed to have belonged to the Scottish ballad-writer Carolina, Baroness Nairne (1766–1845).

▨ PICTURES

4 Stanley Cursiter, *The Queen Receiving the Honours of Scotland, St Giles' Cathedral, Edinburgh, 24 June 1953*, 1954

5 David Donaldson, *Queen Elizabeth II*, 1967

6 Lattanzio Gambara, *Mercury*

7 Lattanzio Gambara, *Apollo*

8 Lattanzio Gambara, *Diana*

9 Lattanzio Gambara, *An Allegory (Fortitude and Charity)*

10 Lattanzio Gambara, *Neptune and Caenis*

11–13 Lattanzio Gambara, *Three Scenes from the Wedding of Pirithöus and Hippodamia*

▨ TAPESTRIES

14 Three Brussels panels from *The Planets* series, late 16th century. Moved from Hampton Court Palace to Holyroodhouse c.1860.
1 The Toilet of Venus
2 Bacchanalian Feast
3 Mars and Venus
Late 16th-century Flemish tapestry from *The Destruction of Troy* series
4 Sinon brought before Priam

▨ ARMS

15 Two cases each containing a trophy of three arrows, presented by the Royal Company of Archers to King Edward VII in 1903, and to King George V in 1911.

16 Two trophies of basket-hilted broadswords, 18th–19th centuries.

THE ROYAL DINING ROOM

▨ FURNITURE

17 Pair of mid-18th-century style giltwood pier tables with marble tops.

18 Pair of mahogany pier tables by Young, Trotter and Hamilton of Edinburgh, part of the large group of furniture made for the apartments of the comte d'Artois in 1796 during his exile at Holyroodhouse.

19 Set of mahogany rail-back dining chairs, late 18th century.

20 Mahogany five-pedestal dining table, early 19th century.

▨ PORCELAIN

21 Part of a Derby porcelain white and gold dessert service, early 19th century.

▨ PICTURES

22 Sir George Hayter, *Queen Victoria in Coronation Robes*, 1838

23 Jens Juel, *Frederik VI, King of Denmark*, 1784

24 Jens Juel, *Louise Augusta, Duchess of Augustenburg*, 1784

25 Sir David Wilkie, *George IV*, 1829

THE THRONE ROOM

ROOM PLAN ➤

THE THRONE ROOM WAS THE SETTING FOR GEORGE IV'S RECEPTIONS ON HIS STATE VISIT IN 1822

THE ANCIENT CROWN OF THE KINGS OF SCOTLAND WAS PRESENTED TO GEORGE IV IN THIS ROOM

THE QUEEN AND THE DUKE OF EDINBURGH GIVE A LUNCH PARTY IN THIS ROOM FOR THE KNIGHTS AND LADIES OF THE ORDER OF THE THISTLE

THE THRONE ROOM has been altered more often than any other room in the palace, changes which can be traced in many historic engravings and photographs. As Charles II's Guardroom it was simply finished with a plain cornice. Then, in 1822, it became the most important room in the palace when it was fitted up as the Great Drawing Room on the occasion of George IV's State Visit to Scotland.

The new Throne Room was hung with crimson cloth with matching 'gorgeous' curtain draperies by the furniture maker William Trotter. The throne and canopy made for Queen Charlotte, mother of George IV, were sent north from what was then known simply as Buckingham House to lend a splash of metropolitan glamour to dowdy Holyroodhouse.

In 1842 the room was rehung with 'crimson merino damask' in anticipation of Queen Victoria's State Visit to Scotland, but after 1850, when the Queen had taken up her residence in the Royal Apartments and Charles II's oak panelling had been stripped of its later white paint, the Throne Room must have appeared modern and tawdry. Although money was always tight, enough cash was found to install a new

Although the present Throne Room has its origins in George IV's visit in 1822, the handsome new furniture provided for the occasion was merely hired from Trotter's and left the palace shortly after the King. The Throne Room's dramatic change of use probably arose because nobody could remember the original room sequence. In the 1822 refitting of the palace, George IV was given exclusive use of the Great Stair while his subjects entered from the east. This was the reverse of Charles II's careful planning. Charles II's ordering of the state rooms at Holyroodhouse followed the general sequence of such rooms in royal palaces, which was itself based upon ancient concepts of formal etiquette and privileged access at both royal and papal courts. At Holyroodhouse the sequence of spaces began with the Guardroom, then the King's Presence Chamber, his Privy Chamber (which, as the name implies, already gave those granted entry to it more private, privileged access to the King than the Presence Chamber), the Ante-Chamber to the bedroom, and then the King's Bedchamber itself.

Queen Charlotte's throne and canopy, photographed *in situ* c.1900.

plaster ceiling bearing the Royal Arms in 1856. This was designed by Robert Matheson in order that the ceiling of this room, which had previously been plain, should 'accord' as a 'continuous suite' with the splendid ceilings of the rooms on either side, and was derived from a seventeenth-century ceiling in an old tower house, the Croft-an-Righ, which still stands in the palace grounds. Its new cornice was intertwined with thistles, roses, lilies and shamrocks, and was modelled by the plasterers John Ramage and Son. It took many years for Queen Victoria to dislodge the persistent grace-and-favour tenants from her palace and thus her Throne Room doubled-up as a dining room until the present Royal Dining Room was released at the end of her reign.

To twentieth-century taste, Matheson's oak-grained ceiling seemed oppressive (Queen Mary described it as 'dreadful'). Although it was claimed that the 'dignity of Scotland' was at stake, it had to be economically painted out in white until money was found to refit the entire room in 1929 to the designs of J. Wilson Paterson of the Office of Works, who wrote in 1931 that:

> the draped canopied Throne, the ribbed ceiling and other early Victorian work was swept away, and finishings appropriate to the Palace and in harmony with the work of Sir William Bruce were substituted. The design of the richly modelled plaster ceiling is based on the lines of other original ones, but care has been taken that it is not in any sense a mere copy, and a modern treatment has been adopted.

Paterson used the new technique of fibrous plasterwork to achieve a convincing imitation of the original Stuart plasterwork, but its date is proclaimed by the monograms of King George V and Queen Mary. In the same spirit, the room was provided with silvered electric chandeliers and wall brackets copied from existing examples in the Royal Collection.

Paterson's new oak panelling, in the Doric order, had to incorporate a number of full-length royal portraits and was installed by Scott Morton and Co, another Edinburgh firm. In the same year Scott Morton also supplied a pair of new thrones for the recess, which was 'cut in the thick wall' to add dignity to the positioning of the thrones in the room. The discarded throne canopy was presented to the National Museums of Scotland but Queen Charlotte's magnificent throne was destroyed when it was found to be infested with woodworm.

Daniel Mytens, *Charles I*, 1628

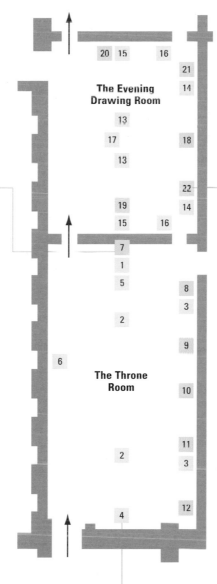

Brussels tapestry after the 17th-century Dutch painter David Teniers, *The Fish Market*, c.1750.

THE THRONE ROOM

FURNITURE

1 Gilt-bronze mantel clock by R. Bryson and Son, Edinburgh, late 19th century.

2 Pair of gilt metal chandeliers by Francis Garthorne, copied from the 18th-century silver originals at Hampton Court Palace.

3 Set of giltwood X-frame stools, 19th century (copying a set made in 1715 by Henry Williams for Hampton Court Palace).

4 Pair of upholstered throne chairs made for King George V and Queen Mary by Morris & Co. of London, 1911.

5 Giltwood side table of 18th-century design.

6 Part of a set of oak window stools with needlework covers made to celebrate the Coronation of King George VI and Queen Elizabeth, 1937.

PICTURES

7 Daniel Mytens, *Charles I*, 1628

8 Sir Peter Lely, *Charles II*, c.1665-70

9 Sir Peter Lely, *Catherine of Braganza*, c.1663 5

10 Paul van Somer, *James VI & I*, 1618

11 Sir Peter Lely, *Mary of Modena when Duchess of York*, c.1675–80

12 Sir Peter Lely, *James VII & II when Duke of York*, c.1665

THE EVENING DRAWING ROOM

FURNITURE

13 Set of six French giltwood armchairs and a sofa by Etienne Saint-Georges, upholstered in Beauvais tapestry woven with La Fontaine's *Fables*, c.1745.

14 Pair of ebonised pier tables with gilt-bronze mounts and marble tops, early 19th century.

15 Pair of gilt gesso side tables, early 18th century.

16 Set of mahogany and parcel-gilt side chairs, mid 18th century. Formerly in the Fitzwilliam Collection, Wentworth Woodhouse.

17 Silver-plated chandelier by Francis Garthorne, copied from the 18th-century silver original at Hampton Court Palace.

PICTURES

18 Sir William Hutchinson, *Queen Elizabeth The Queen Mother*, 1967

TAPESTRIES

Two Brussels panels from a set of *The Four Continents*, workshop of Peter and Franz van der Borght, c.1750. Formerly at Buckingham Palace.
19 Asia
20 Africa

Two Brussels 'Teniers' panels, workshop of Franz van der Borght, c.1750. Formerly at Buckingham Palace.
21 The Vegetable Market
22 The Fish Market

Pair of upholstered throne chairs made for King George V and Queen Mary in 1911.

33

THE EVENING DRAWING ROOM

THE NEXT FIVE ROOMS of the King's Apartment retain most of their Carolean decoration, which builds up to a climax in the King's Bedchamber.

The Evening Drawing Room was originally Charles II's Presence Chamber. Houlbert and Dunsterfield's plaster ceiling here has particularly vigorous, almost whiplash, whirling scrolls, set against panels of interwoven laurel branches, but the effect is again weakened without the intended decorative painting in the central quatrefoil panel. The red marble chimneypiece is the first of a series in a deliberately varied selection of exotic marbles used in the palace. They were purchased by an agent of the Duke of Lauderdale in London and contribute to the effect of baroque opulence.

This room was modernised with wallpaper in the late eighteenth century, and after Queen Victoria's return to London following her State Visit, the four panels of Brussels tapestry in the room were sent up from Buckingham Palace in 1851 to give it an extra air of richness and warmth. In the Victorian era this room was used by the Court as a general sitting room.

During King George V's renovations the eighteenth-century wallpaper was replaced with oak, and the Victorian plate-glass windows were refitted with their original small panes and astragals. Unfortunately the architects of the Office of Works, in their zeal to create a neo-Carolean character, mistakenly also disposed of the pair of genuine Carolean Ionic pilasters which used to frame the chimneypiece.

THE EVENING DRAWING ROOM
CONTAINS ONE OF THE FINEST
CEILINGS IN THE PALACE

THE FOUR TAPESTRIES IN THE ROOM
WERE SENT UP FROM BUCKINGHAM
PALACE IN 1851

IN QUEEN VICTORIA'S TIME, THE
COURT USED THIS ROOM AS THEIR
DRAWING ROOM

IN CHARLES II'S PALACE IT WAS THE
KING'S PRESENCE CHAMBER

THE MORNING DRAWING ROOM

ROOM PLAN →

THE MORNING DRAWING ROOM was Charles II's Privy Chamber. The increasing richness of its decoration indicates the ever more exclusive character of each successive interior on the progression through the King's Apartment. To underline this sense of entering ever richer rooms, Bruce selected the more ornate Corinthian order for the pilasters here. These frame the dark green marble chimneypiece and support an appropriately enriched Corinthian entablature above it, which breaks forward over the pilasters and then continues around the room as the cornice. The pedestals which support the pilasters are also continued round the room, as the dado.

This highly disciplined architectural effect, so characteristic of Bruce, was emulated in the state rooms of many of Scotland's castles and country houses as the fashions set at Holyroodhouse were copied throughout the land. However, only the Duke of Lauderdale, at Thirlestane Castle, managed to achieve anything like the richness of Houlbert and Dunsterfield's astounding illusionistic plasterwork in this room, where the swags surrounding the central compartment are apparently held to the ceiling only by ribbons. In the corners of the ceiling the King's wreathed cypher (see detail illustrated overleaf) is borne aloft by eagles and cherubs, while heraldic lions and unicorns spring from delicately modelled roseheads in the long central panels.

The French tapestries in this room illustrate the story of Diana, the goddess of hunting, and cost £90 when they were purchased for Charles II in 1668 from the Edinburgh merchant John Coupar. They were well suited to the antiquarian mood cultivated in the renovations undertaken in 1850 for Queen Victoria. The Edinburgh decorator D. R. Hay painted the ceiling in rich colours to complement the tapestries. After the intervention of the 10th Duke of Hamilton 'with his superior taste and great experience in his own magnificent palace', enough money was released to further embellish the ceiling with gilding. De Wet's painting was deemed unsuitable, however, and was covered over with mirror glass. Hay's own ceiling was deemed to be in doubtful taste after King George V's State Visit in 1911, and was painted out in white during the later general de-Victorianisation of the palace.

THE TAPESTRIES IN THIS ROOM HAVE HUNG HERE SINCE AT LEAST 1796

QUEEN VICTORIA USED THIS ROOM AS HER PRIVATE DRAWING ROOM

TODAY THE QUEEN GIVES AUDIENCES IN THIS ROOM

MAHOGANY SETTEE covered with silk and wool embroidery, c.1740.

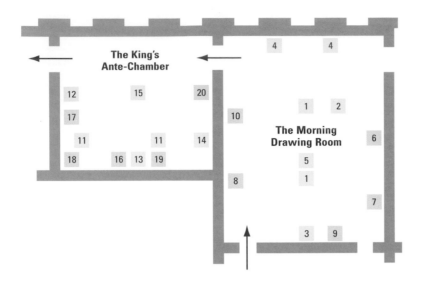

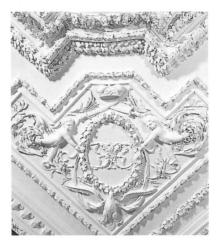

Detail of the plasterwork of the ceiling in the Morning Drawing Room, showing the butterfly-shaped cypher of Charles II.

THE MORNING DRAWING ROOM

FURNITURE

1 Set of mahogany side chairs with canvas-work embroidery, mid-18th century. The set was extended and new needlework panels made in the 1920s by a group of ladies of Scotland for Queen Mary.

2 Mahogany tripod polescreen with contemporary needlework, mid-18th century.

3 Mahogany settee covered with canvas-work embroidery in silk and wool, c.1740.

4 Pair of giltwood pier tables and glasses, the tables with the arms and heraldic supporters of the Duchess of Gordon, mother of Lord Adam Gordon, c.1770. Recorded at Holyroodhouse since 1782.

5 Silver-plated chandelier by Francis Garthorne, copied from the 18th-century silver original at Hampton Court Palace.

PICTURES

6 Jacob de Wet, *Morning at the Bath*, c.1675

TAPESTRIES

Three French (Paris) panels from *The History of Diana*, c.1630.
7 Niobe protests at the worship of Latona
8 Diana petitioning Jupiter
9 Actaeon turned into a stag

10 Flemish panel of Tobit and Anna, early 17th century.

The chimneypiece in the Morning Drawing Room. The chimneypiece is enriched with lively carving by the Dutch sculptor Jan van Santvoort, which frames a decorative painting by Jacob de Wet traditionally entitled *Cupid and Psyche*, but now thought more likely to depict *Morning at the Bath*.

THE KING'S ANTE-CHAMBER

FURNITURE

11 Ten ebonised side chairs upholstered in modern red velvet, late 17th century. Formerly in the Paulet collection, Hinton House, Somerset.

12 German marquetry cabinet, late 16th century, on later English walnut stand.

13 Oyster-veneered walnut cabinet on stand, late 17th century.

14 Walnut writing table, late 17th century. Similar to a table made for William III at Hampton Court Palace.

15 Cut-glass eight-branch chandelier, mid-18th century.

TAPESTRIES

Two Flemish panels of *The Aeneid*, late 16th century. Recorded at Holyroodhouse since 1685.
16 The death of Dido
17 The meeting of Dido and Aeneas (fragment)

Two French (Paris) panels from the *History of Diana*, c.1630 (*en suite* with the three in the Morning Drawing Room)
18 The destruction of the children of Niobe
19 Diana with her nymphs

PICTURES

20 Jacob de Wet, *The Triumph of Galatea*, c.1675

THE KING'S ANTE-CHAMBER

ALTHOUGH THIS ROOM, with its pink and white marble chimneypiece, is richly decorated, the plasterwork is more restrained to suit the smaller scale and function of the room. It has an overmantel painting by De Wet of *The Triumph of Galatea* but the central panel of the ceiling again lacks its decorative painting and attention thus rests on the grotesque clawed monsters in the corners of the ceiling, and the illusionistic plaster ribbons threaded through its mouldings. This room was Queen Victoria's bedroom in 1850, but after the death of the Prince Consort she withdrew to a suite on the floor above – once it had been vacated by its grace-and-favour tenant, the Duke of Argyll, in 1871.

THE KING'S BEDCHAMBER

ROOM PLAN ➤

THE KING'S BEDCHAMBER IS THE MOST
ELABORATELY DECORATED IN THE
PALACE

THE CEILING CONTAINS AN
ILLUSIONISTIC CENTRAL PAINTING
BY JACOB DE WET

PRINCE ALBERT, THE PRINCE CONSORT,
USED THIS ROOM AS HIS DRESSING
ROOM

THE SUPREMACY OF THIS ROOM is made clear not only in the elaboration of its decoration – it contains the finest plasterwork, decorative painting and carving in the palace – but also through its position on the central axis of the building, like Louis XIV's bedroom at the French royal palace of Versailles. This axial thrust would have been continued by the new Privy Garden to the east which, at Charles II's suggestion, this room was to overlook.

This is the only ceiling in the palace to have been completed with an illusionistic decorative painting, *Hercules Admitted to Olympus* (illustrated overleaf). Here, De Wet strove to give the viewer the impression of looking up into a realistic sky, but one peopled with gods. The menagerie of animals who totter precariously on the brink to peer down into the room add to the illusion and include owls and sheep – plus, perhaps, what were intended as a pair of King Charles's spaniels. To add to the overall richness of the ceiling the motifs in the corners are counter-changed (that is, with contrasting paired motifs) rather than being identical, and the crowned Thistle of Scotland makes its first appearance.

De Wet followed his flattering comparison of Charles II with Hercules through into his overmantel painting, where this toughest of infants is seen strangling one of the serpents sent to slay him in his cot. The luxuriance of the materials in this room is echoed by Hercules' golden cradle and the antique-style silver chair of his nursemaid,

THE STATE BED IN THE KING'S BEDCHAMBER. This was the bed exhibited by the Duke of Hamilton's servants in their tours of Mary, Queen of Scots' Chambers as 'the couch of the Rose of Scotland'. In fact it dates from c.1680.

Jacob de Wet, *The Infant Hercules Strangling the Serpents*, c.1675

George M. Greig, *The Prince Consort's sitting room and dressing room*, 1863. Prince Albert's shower-bath is on the left, and his slippers can be seen by the chaise-longue.

which would not have seemed as exotic to Charles II as it does today since, like Louis XIV, the king possessed his own silver mirror and tables. The sculpted surround of the overmantel and the lions framing the fawn marble chimneypiece are every bit as deeply undercut as the plasterwork, and the present draperies give a good impression of the rich embroidery which would have been seen on the King's State Bed.

The panelling is no less ornamented than the rest, while the formality of the room is underlined by strong vertical emphases created by the continued over-doors with their octagonal panels. This dark oak panelling has never been bleached, unlike that in the preceding rooms, but its depth of colour may be due to Trotter's workmen, who stripped it of its late eighteenth-century white paint in 1850 and high-varnished it. The eighteenth-century six-panelled doors must have replaced the original lug-panelled doors, such as those seen in the Queen's Apartment (see pages 50-53). That in the west wall leads to the King's Dressing Room.

From 1850 until his death in 1861 this room was the Prince Consort's Dressing Room. A contemporary watercolour shows his portable shower-bath installed in a corner of the room. In 1976 it was decided to display this room as a baroque royal bedroom, using the late seventeenth-century State Bed and furnishings from the Duke of Hamilton's apartments.

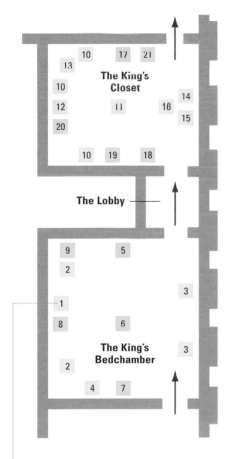

Detail of the ceiling painting in the King's Bedchamber by Jacob de Wet, *Hercules Admitted to Olympus*, 1675.

TAPESTRIES

Two mid-17th-century Brussels panels of *The History of Alexander*, workshop of Jan Leyniers. Recorded at Holyroodhouse from before 1700.
7 Alexander wounded in the thigh
8 The Lion Hunt

9 Flemish 17th-century panel from the *Diogenes* series: Diogenes writing on the wall

THE KING'S BEDCHAMBER

FURNITURE

1 State Bed with crimson damask upholstery (largely renewed), c.1680.

2 Four lacquered and ebonised armchairs and one side chair with modern upholstery, late 17th century.

3 Two walnut pier tables, two walnut mirrors and two pairs of walnut candlestands, late 17th century.

4 Walnut longcase clock by J. Windmills, London, early 18th century.

PICTURES

5 Jacob de Wet, *The Infant Hercules Strangling the Serpents*, c.1675

6 Jacob de Wet, *Hercules Admitted to Olympus*, 1675

THE KING'S CLOSET

FURNITURE

10 Five lacquered and ebonised chairs with modern green damask upholstery, late 17th century.

11 Lacquered two manual harpsichord with false inscription of Johannes Ruckers of Antwerp, and date of 1636. French, mid-18th century.

12 Chinese lacquer cabinet, 18th century, on later ebonised stand.

13 Black lacquered and gilt harp by Holtzman, Paris, early 19th century.

14 Pair of carved and giltwood candlestands, late 17th century.

15 Ebonised and silvered pier table with mermaid and dolphin legs, late 17th century.

16 Carved limewood pier glass, late 17th century.

PICTURES

17 Jacob de Wet, *The Finding of Moses*, c.1675

TAPESTRIES

Four English (Mortlake) panels of *The Life of Diogenes*, late 17th century. Purchased for Charles II in 1683.
18 Diogenes visited by Plato
19 Diogenes meditating
20 The meeting of Alexander and Diogenes
21 Diogenes beside his barrel

Detail of the head board of the State Bed.

43

THE LOBBY

THE LITTLE LOBBY led to the King's Stool Room, which contained only his close-stool (or water-closet), but its decoration is no less rich or carefully considered. The borrowed light appears to be original and lights a mezzanine which may have been intended for the King's valet. In 1850 it was certainly being occupied by Prince Albert's valet. In the same year, D. R. Hay painted the miniature dome, with its vases of flowers in the spandrels, 'deep azure', and sprinkled it with silver stars, but it has now been painted white.

THE KING'S CLOSET

THE PRIVATE CHARACTER OF THIS SMALL ROOM is made clear in the intimate effect created by the coved ceiling. The spandrels of the ceiling are appropriately decorated for a king's private study with military trophies and this theme continues through into the antique armour framing the overmantel, which projects boldly into the room. In the coving, with its shell corners, the Royal Arms of Scotland are paired with fantastic cartouches in which Charles II's cypher is supported by naked figures. De Wet's overmantel painting depicts *The Finding of Moses* and alludes to the mythical descent of the Scottish kings from Pharaoh's daughter, Scota.

In 1850 this room became Queen Victoria's Breakfast Room, and was hung with green and gold flock wallpaper.

THE KING'S CLOSET, showing the mid-18th-century harpsichord, and a 19th-century harp, with on the wall behind them a late 17th-century Mortlake tapestry, one of four in the room.

THE GREAT GALLERY.
During Charles X's first sojourn at the palace, as the exiled comte d'Artois, a Catholic chapel was established in the Great Gallery.
It has also been used for the election of delegates for Westminster from among Scotland's peers; by tradition, Bonnie Prince Charlie gave a ball here; and Cumberland's troops were quartered here. It is now used for state banquets.

THE GREAT GALLERY

THE GREAT GALLERY CONTAINS JACOB DE WET'S 110 PORTRAITS OF REAL AND LEGENDARY KINGS OF SCOTLAND, FROM FERGUS I TO CHARLES II

THE ROOM IS 44.5 METRES (124 FEET) LONG, AND IS THE LARGEST IN THE PALACE

THE QUEEN AND THE DUKE OF EDINBURGH ENTERTAIN VISITING HEADS OF STATE TO STATE BANQUETS IN THIS ROOM

THE GREAT GALLERY connects the King's new Apartment in the east section of the palace with the Queen's rooms in the old Royal Apartment to the west (in James V's Tower). Certain irregularities in its form suggest that it incorporates earlier walls, and the close proximity of the abbey is apparent in the cluster of buttresses obscuring the east windows.

Sir William Bruce devised a simple classical scheme for the Great Gallery, with Doric surrounds to the pair of black marble chimneypieces. These are framed by Ionic pilasters, supporting a cornice enriched with scrollwork and figures. However, the unique decorative character of the Gallery was established in February 1684, when De Wet was contracted to supply the portraits of the 110 real and legendary kings of Scotland. The origins of the commission for this important sequence of portraits, which took De Wet two years to complete, are far from clear.

The Great Gallery, with tables laid for a
state banquet.

Tam O'Shanter chair, early 19th century.
Acquired by George IV in 1822 and sent to
Holyroodhouse by King Edward VII in 1901.

A formative influence must have been the similar series known to have been painted by the artist George Jamieson (c.1587-1644) to decorate one of the triumphal arches erected in honour of Charles I's coronation in Edinburgh in 1633. De Wet certainly drew on Jamieson's series, but there seem to have been established likenesses for all the Scottish kings from the accession of James I in 1406. Inevitably, given the dynastic function it was intended to fulfil, the contract for the series attached as much importance to the inscriptions bearing each king's 'name, age, the years of reign and date of the world' as to any concept of reliable portraiture.

The series seem to have been conceived as freely hanging paintings because there was no attempt to relate them in size to the panels over the chimneypieces or the over-doors. Charles II is depicted standing next to a fantastic table with muscular gilded legs, terminating in claw and ball feet and topped with eagles' heads, which might reflect something of the character of the furnishings of his new Scottish palace, had it ever been completed.

The paintings are said to have been 'slashed by the sabres' of English troops quartered in the palace after the 1745 Rebellion and archaeological evidence during conservation has confirmed this. Especial violence was reserved for the portrait of Mary, Queen of Scots. By 1826 they had been 'repaired; and after having been removed from their hanging frames, fixed in the panels of the wainscoting' – but a number still hung loose in the window-embrasures at the end of the nineteenth century.

The Great Gallery is the largest room in the palace, and has served many purposes. After the Union of the Parliaments in 1707, it was used for the election of delegates from among Scotland's representative peers to attend Parliament in Westminster, and tradition has it that Bonnie Prince Charlie gave a ball here in 1745. King George V improved the service arrangements in the rooms to the north and made it into the State Dining Room. Screens covered with tapestry were 'placed at the ends of the table to shorten the room'. When the floors of the rooms above were strengthened in 1968, the opportunity was taken to install a new ornamental ceiling to take away the previous tunnel-like appearance of the room. Designed by George Hay, it was executed by Albert Cram.

49

THE QUEEN'S LOBBY

THE NEXT THREE ROOMS (once known as the 'Darnley Rooms') comprise the old Royal Apartment in James V's Tower, refitted in 1671 to serve as the Queen's Apartment. Although the rooms were old and irregular, Bruce was no less anxious to impose architectural order on them. A new marble chimneypiece was framed by a pair of Ionic pilasters and the vertical emphasis followed through, as before in the King's Bedchamber, in the overmantel and over-doors. Despite this, the character of these rooms remains simple, almost vernacular, especially in comparison with the baroque splendours of the King's Apartment. Because no queen ever came to use these rooms, they were appropriated by the Duke and Duchess of Hamilton. From time to time they were modernised by the introduction of paper hangings and more fashionable furniture. Outmoded furniture, some of it from the baroque period, was relegated to the less important rooms on the upper floor of the Tower, where the Hamiltons' servants recycled it for their re-tellings of the history of Mary, Queen of Scots.

In 1855, after Queen Victoria's return to the palace, responsibility for showing the 'Historical Apartments' was assumed by the Office of Works, and the Duke of Hamilton moved to new apartments above the Great Gallery. His old first-floor rooms were redecorated in a deliberately antiquarian mode, to harmonise with those of Mary, Queen of Scots above, and old furniture and tapestry was collected to replace the more modern paper hangings.

Bog-oak chair from the Queen's Apartment. The chair was made in 1850 by Curran and Sons of Lisburn from oak found in 1848 at Carr Moss, Co. Down.

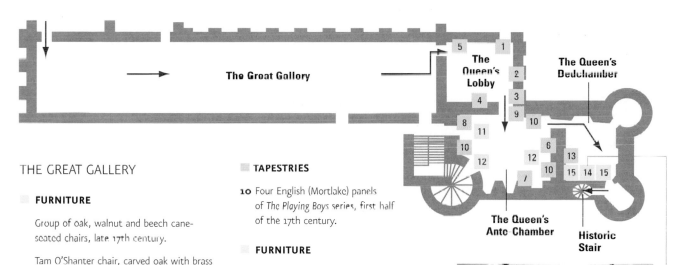

THE GREAT GALLERY

FURNITURE

Group of oak, walnut and beech cane-seated chairs, late 17th century.

Tam O'Shanter chair, carved oak with brass panels, early 19th century.

PICTURES

Jacob de Wet: 110 individual portraits of the rulers of Scotland from Fergus I to Charles II, 1684.

THE QUEEN'S LOBBY

PICTURES

1 Sir Peter Lely, *Princess Isabella*, c.1677 (over-door)

2 Alexis-Simon Belle, *Prince James Francis Edward Stuart with his sister, Princess Louisa Maria Theresa*, 1699

3 ?after Alexis-Simon Belle, *Prince James Francis Edward Stuart*, 18th century

4 Francesco Trevisani, *Prince James Francis Edward Stuart*, 1719 (overmantel)

5 ?Alexis-Simon Belle, *Prince James Francis Edward Stuart*, c.1705 (over-door)

THE QUEEN'S ANTE-CHAMBER

PICTURES

6 Adriaen Hanneman, *William Hamilton, Earl of Lanark and 2nd Duke of Hamilton*, 1650

7 North Italian School, *James 'the Admirable' Crichton*, c.1580

8 British School, *An Incident in the Rebellion of 1745*, c.1745–50

9 Francesco Fieravino, *Still life of Fruit and Flowers with a Carpet*, c.1650 (over-door)

TAPESTRIES

10 Four English (Mortlake) panels of *The Playing Boys* series, first half of the 17th century.

FURNITURE

11 Dutch marquetry centre table, 19th century.

12 Part of a group of walnut or beech side chairs with original Turkey-work upholstery, late 17th century. Bought for Holyroodhouse by the Earl of Lauderdale in 1668 (see below).

THE QUEEN'S BEDCHAMBER

PICTURES

13 William Wissing, *Posthumous Portrait of James, Duke of Cambridge*, c.1685 (overmantel)

FURNITURE

14 Tester bed upholstered in crimson and gold velvet and yellow satin (part renewed), c.1682.

15 Two ebonised wing chairs, modern upholstery, late 17th century.

Two chairs with original Turkey-work upholstery, late 17th century.

Detail of the tester bed in the Queen's Bedchamber. The quality of its fringes, which incorporate silk-covered wire flowers in baskets, has only become apparent since recent conservation. When Bonnie Prince Charlie occupied the Duke of Hamilton's Apartments at Holyroodhouse in 1745 this is the bed he slept in, only to be succeeded in it shortly afterwards by the victorious Duke of Cumberland.

HISTORIC STAIR

PICTURES

William Aikman, *John Campbell, 2nd Duke of Argyll and Duke of Greenwich*, c.1709

THE QUEEN'S ANTE-CHAMBER AND BEDCHAMBER

MORTLAKE TAPESTRY, *The Playing Boys* (detail; from a series of four). Part of the remarkable collection of furniture assembled by the lawyer and antiquarian R. G. Ellis and acquired by Robert Matheson in 1864.

SOMEWHAT CONFUSINGLY, the rooms now known as the Queen's Ante-Chamber and the Queen's Bedchamber comprise what was the original King's Apartment in James V's Tower. These rooms were refitted by Bruce after 1671 but they still retain a Scottish vernacular character, and the great thickness of the walls betrays the building's defensive origins. The black marble chimneypiece is framed by a pair of Ionic pilasters but although the new ceiling looks like those in the King's Apartment, it is of old-fashioned cast, rather than hand-modelled, plaster. The doors have characteristic Scottish lugged panels, and overall the effect of the room is simpler than that of Charles II's King's Apartment.

During the eighteenth century this room became the Duke of Hamilton's dining room, and was furnished with handsome early Georgian furniture. After the Office of Works assumed responsibility for showing these rooms in 1855, and despite the fact that they had the interest of being in the most ancient part of the palace, their modern ceilings and fittings must have made them seem dull.

It was in this room that Darnley and his co-conspirators met on the night of the murder of David Rizzio.

The Queen's Bedchamber was the original King's Bedroom of James V's Tower. In 1528 the two additional inner rooms provided in the round corner towers must have seemed the height of planning sophistication, but by the standards of a queen in 1671, the accommodation was inadequate. Additional service rooms were therefore provided in a wing which joined the Tower to the north. Even Bruce was unable to impose much regularity on the Queen's Bedchamber, but he characteristically built up the sense of increasing grandeur, partly by framing the chimneypiece with Corinthian pilasters to indicate the room's importance.

In 1740, following his marriage to his third wife in 1738, the Duke of Hamilton carried out extensive renovations to this room. The Duchess was given a fashionable new bedroom in the adjacent wing, designed by the architect William Adam, and the existing rooms were refurnished in the latest style. Unfortunately the wing was demolished during George IV's improvements after 1822, and thus the characteristic dove-coloured chimneypiece supplied by William Adam's marble works for this room is the sole survivor of this elegant transformation.

The bed now shown in this room was moved here in the early twentieth century when Mary, Queen of Scots' Outer Chamber on the floor above was renovated. For almost a century it had been passed off as Charles I's bed, but was probably supplied by John Ridge, a London upholsterer, to the Duke of Hamilton in 1682. In that year the Duke paid '£218. 10s. 0d' for 'a crimson and gould velvet bed, lined with satin with 8 chairs and velvet cases, a feather bed and bolster, quilts Japanned glass and stands a footstool, blankets ...'

Early 17th-century oak veneered
Flemish cabinet from the Queen's
Apartment. The marquetry decoration
shows scenes of architectural ruins and
warriors on horseback.

THES BE THE SONES OF 'FF RIGHT HONERABLES TEFLLE OF LENOXE AD TE LADY MARGARETZ GRACE COVNTYES OF LENOXE AD ANGWYSE.

1563

CHARLLES STEWARDE HIS BROTHER. ÆTATIS. 6.   HENRY STEWARDE LORD DARLEY AND DOWGLAS. ÆTATIS 17.

Attributed to Hans Eworth, *Henry Stuart, Lord Darnley, and his brother Charles, 5th Earl of Lennox*, c.1562. This portrait can be seen in Mary, Queen of Scots' Outer Chamber.
After Darnley's death, his mother the Countess of Lennox commissioned the Darnley Jewel in memory of her son and her husband.
The jewel is one of the great treasures of Holyroodhouse and is illustrated on page 60. When it is on show to visitors it is also exhibited in the Outer Chamber.

A 17TH-CENTURY FLEMISH CABINET veneered in red tortoiseshell with silver and silver-gilt mounts, on a 19th-century stand, inscribed as having belonged to Mary, Queen of Scots.

adjoining Outer Chamber, stabbed a total of 56 times, and left dying on the threshold of the room.

Eleven months later, Darnley himself was dead – found strangled after a mysterious explosion at the house in Edinburgh where he had been staying. Mary, whose estrangement from her husband was common knowledge, married James Hepburn, 4th Earl of Bothwell, at Holyroodhouse on 15 May 1567. The marriage was universally condemned, both by the Pope and the Scottish nobility, and on 24 July Mary was forced to abdicate in favour of her one-year-old son. A year later she fled to England.

Early nineteenth-century guidebooks to Holyroodhouse were at pains to persuade visitors that the rooms had remained untouched and complete with their original furniture (and Rizzio's bloodstains) since this night of 'sorrow and crime'. In fact the air of apparent antiquity of Mary, Queen of Scots' Chambers has a different explanation.

During Bruce's remodelling of the palace, the Queen's Apartments were relocated on the floor below, and the original second-floor rooms lost their importance (thus although they were given new timber chimneypieces, their old-fashioned geometric oak ceilings, which may date back to the mid-sixteenth century, were retained, reflecting the rooms' demotion). In the absence of a resident Queen, the rooms were then appropriated by the Dukes of Hamilton, who had previously been accommodated in the gatehouse, and who introduced sumptuous baroque furniture into their rooms here, including the famous red damask State Bed. By the mid-eighteenth century, the attention of visitors to the palace had shifted from Charles II's improvements and alterations, which were now deemed unfashionable, to focus on the growing romantic cult of Mary, Queen of Scots. Her rooms, with their ancient heraldic ceilings, thick walls and gloomy spiral staircases, in combination with the details of the murder, exerted a powerful visual and theatrical appeal. Successive editions of the same standard guidebook from this period reveal how the Hamilton's baroque furniture gradually came to be passed off to visitors as that of Mary, Queen of Scots. And as these rooms fell out of ordinary domestic use, due to their new role as a tourist attraction, there was no incentive to repair the furnishings, which were allowed to moulder into an ever-more romantic decay.

By the time of the accession of King Edward VII in 1901, this exaggerated cult of decay had not only begun to look more like real neglect, but scholarship in furniture history had developed to the point where it was embarrassingly obvious that the much-venerated red damask bed, which Sir Walter Scott had poetically described as the 'couch of the Rose of Scotland', could not possibly be earlier in date that the late seventeenth century, thus missing Mary, Queen of Scots by some 120 years. Through a succession of repairs to the rooms, and the eventual re-upholstering of the bedstead itself in a modern silk, the seductive visual appeal of the rooms, which had attracted

LEFT: MARY, QUEEN OF SCOTS' OUTER CHAMBER in an oil painting of c.1880. The State Bed of c.1680, now in the King's Bedchamber, is clearly recognisable.

Francois Clouet, *Mary, Queen of Scots in White Mourning*, 1559-61. In the space of eighteen months Mary lost her father-in-law, her mother and her husband.

generations of artists and visitors, was lost. In the mid-1970s, acting on the advice of the Victoria and Albert Museum, the decision was taken to strip these rooms back to their antiquarian essentials and relocate the Hamiltons' baroque furniture in Charles II's contemporary King's Apartment. One great advantage of this was to allow the conservation and display of the painted *trompe-l'oeil* grisaille frieze, thought to have been executed in 1617 in preparation for the visit of James VI and I.

In recent years, the Royal Collection has assumed responsibility for showing these rooms, and the development of a renewed interest in antiquarianism has led to a new appreciation of the importance of their later history. In 1994 the designer Alec Cobbe was therefore commissioned to make these rooms a more enjoyable experience for visitors, guided by the many paintings and engravings of them. A new bed was created from old materials in the palace's historic collections and furniture and paintings introduced from the Royal Collection in order to bring back something of the theatrical visual appeal and antiquarian effect these celebrated interiors had given to so many generations of visitors.

Detail of the ceiling of Mary, Queen of Scots' Bedchamber. The initials were probably added to the panels in 1617, in preparation for James VI and I's visit to Scotland. They commemorate Mary, Queen of Scots' first marriage to Francis II of France, and may have been carved some years earlier, in 1558.

17TH-CENTURY STUMPWORK CASKET, known as the Little Gidding Casket, and said in the 19th century to have been the property of Mary, Queen of Scots.

MARY, QUEEN OF SCOTS' OUTER CHAMBER

THIS ROOM was celebrated by generations of tourists to Scotland as it was reputed to retain traces on the floorboards of the actual bloodstains from the murder of Rizzio. During the Edwardian refurbishment, a tame inscribed brass plate was installed. It is also related that this room was the scene of John Knox's interview with Mary, Queen of Scots when the Protestant reformer 'inveighed against the errors' of his Catholic Queen. The oak ceiling, restored in the early twentieth century, records in its heraldry the marriage of Mary, Queen of Scots to the future Francis II of France, but the attractive old blue-and-white tiles in the fireplaces here and elsewhere in the palace were also introduced during the Edwardian improvements.

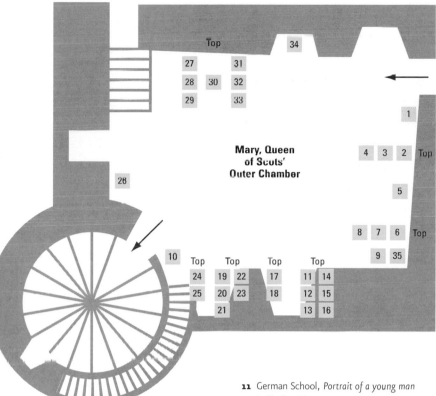

26 British School, *A memorial painting of Charles I*, 17th century

27 Follower of Jacopo Bassano, *A mysterious appearance of a female saint*, c.1560

28 Ippolito Scarsellino, *The Tribute Money*, c.1615

29 Style of Adriaen van der Werff, *Adam and Eve*, c.1700

30 Flemish School, *The Family of Henry VII with St George and the Dragon*, c.1507

31 After Raphael, *The Holy Family with St John*, c.1660

32 North Italian School, *Head of Christ*, c.1525

33 Follower of Giovanni Bellini, *Head of a woman*, c.1510

34 Livinus de Vogelaare, *The Memorial of Lord Darnley*, c.1567

35 Painted plaster bust of Charles I, the face after Gianlorenzo Bernini, late 17th century

■ TAPESTRIES

Five Flemish verdure or forest panels, late 17th century

THE STUART RELICS

The *objets d'art* in the display cabinets are individually labelled. A selection is illustrated overleaf.

Needlework panel worked by Mary, Queen of Scots. The panel dates from the period 1569-84, when Mary was in captivity in England, and shows her *MA* cypher to the right of the cat's head.

MARY, QUEEN OF SCOTS' OUTER CHAMBER

■ PICTURES AND SCULPTURE

1 Alexander Fraser, *Mary, Queen of Scots' bedroom, Holyroodhouse*, c.1884

2 Niccolò dell'Abate, *Portrait of a young man with a cleft chin*, c.1540

3 After Paul van Somer, *James VI and I*, c.1620

4 Manner of Remigius van Leemput, *Portrait of a woman*, c.1645

5 British School, *Mary, Queen of Scots*, 18th century

6 Follower of Francesco Salviati, *Giovanni della Casa*, c.1550

7 British School, *'Mr George'*, 1617

8 Workshop of Bernard van Orley, *Isabella of Austria*, c.1520

9 Attributed to Hans Eworth, *Henry Stuart, Lord Darnley and his brother Charles, 5th Earl of Lennox*, c.1562

10 British School, *Portrait of a woman*, 17th century

11 German School, *Portrait of a young man in black*, 16th century

12 British School, *Catherine of Aragon*, 16th century

13 Flemish School, *Emperor Charles V as a child*, c.1510

14 Flemish School, *Maria, Queen of Hungary*, 16th century

15 British School, *Anne Boleyn*, 16th century

16 Attributed to Pieter van Coninxloo, *Portrait of a lady, possibly Jeanne de Beersel, Countess of Zollern*, c.1510-15

17 After Titian, *Philip II, King of Spain*, c.1620

18 After Anthonis Mor, *Mary I*, c.1600

19 British School, *Henry VII*, 16th century

20 British School, *Portrait of a woman*, 16th century

21 Attributed to Cornelus Ketel, *Portrait of a young man aged 23*, c.1600-1650

22 After Hans Holbein the Younger, *Henry VIII*, c.1600

23 After William Scrots, *Edward VI*, c.1600

24 Attributed to Christobal de Morales, *Sebastian, King of Portugal*, c.1565

25 British School, *Portrait of a man, known as David Rizzio*, 17th century

THE DARNLEY JEWEL, C.1570. The jewel – in fact a locket – is made of gold and enamel, and set with a large false sapphire, rubies and an emerald. Some of the decoration alludes to the Countess of Lennox's hope that her grandson James would succeed to the throne of England. The Darnley Jewel was bought by Queen Victoria in May 1842.

SILVER-GILT CADDINET of Henry Benedict, Cardinal York, made in Rome by L. Valadier, c.1785–90. The caddinet was intended to be used for ceremonial dining.

Mary, Queen of Scots' Outer Chamber is devoted to a display of the Royal Family's extensive collection of Stuart and Jacobite relics, which had been collected by or presented to successive sovereigns. These were gathered together by Queen Mary into one room at Windsor Castle, known as the Stuart Collection. They came to Holyroodhouse in 1995 and are now displayed in cases designed by Alec Cobbe which draw on the early seventeenth-century Scottish fashion for extravagant funerary monuments. The cult of Mary, Queen of Scots had led to the preservation of many early treasures of outstanding aesthetic and historical importance, such as the Darnley Jewel, but as with the legend of the 'couch of the Rose of Scotland', had embraced many objects of more doubtful authenticity, such as the 'Darnley armour'. The collection also includes relics of the later Stuarts, such as the silver-gilt caddinet made in Rome for Cardinal York, the brother of Bonnie Prince Charlie. Modern museum labelling would have been inappropriate for this lively and varied collection of relics, some of which require a degree of faith on the part of the beholder, so hand-written labels were produced in order to continue the antiquarian tradition.

Sixteenth-century Flemish or English silver pomander, said to have belonged to Mary, Queen of Scots.

THE ABBEY CHURCH

MARY, QUEEN OF SCOTS MARRIED BOTH
LORD DARNLEY AND HER THIRD
HUSBAND, THE 4TH EARL OF BOTHWELL,
IN THE ABBEY CHURCH

THE ABBEY CHURCH NOW CONTAINS
THE REMAINS OF JAMES V AND
MADELEINE OF VALOIS AMONG OTHER
ROYAL BURIALS

THE STARTLING WAY IN WHICH THE REMAINS of the abbey collide with the rearing bulk of the palace demonstrate how the original religious foundation was subsumed by the needs of the royal residence. Only the nave of the Abbey Church has survived, but in 1910–11, the site of the transepts and choir was excavated by the Office of Works and their foundations left exposed in the lawn to allow the extent of the abbey to be more readily visualised.

Building work on the church must have begun soon after its foundation by David I in 1128. The processional door leading from the cloisters is the sole surviving feature of this first church as a renewed building programme between c.1195 and c.1230 replaced the first modest structure with an ambitious cathedral-sized building. This was built around the existing walls, enabling the early church to continue in use until most of the grand new design was in place, at which point the early work was demolished.

The interior of the north wall of the nave was given distinctive interlaced arcades, although the style changed as work advanced, and the west front was richly articulated around the deeply recessed and highly ornamented west door. To create an impressive frontage facing Edinburgh, the width of the west façade was increased by two very large square towers, extending beyond the walls of the nave. The southern tower was later absorbed by the palace but the surviving tower still dominates the view down the Canongate. The ambition of the builders is also shown by their decision to vault over the nave in stone, but only the southernmost line of vaulting survived the collapse of the roof in 1768.

There may have been an inherent instability in the building which gave rise to difficulties at an early date because Abbot Crawford (1460–83) had already added flying buttresses to it. The frequent destructive raids by English armies must also have wrought havoc through the years. In the 'Rough-Wooing' raid of 1544, when Henry VIII was trying to force the Scots to accept a marriage between his son and the infant Mary, Queen of Scots, Sir Richard Lee looted the lectern of the abbey. This had been a gift from Abbot George Crichton, and was subsequently presented to the parish church of St Stephen at St Albans in Hertfordshire. It was thus the only fitting of the abbey to come through the destruction of the Reformation unscathed. The nave owed its survival during the same period to its adoption as the parish church for the Burgh of the Canongate. However the remains of the eastern portions of the abbey appear to have been cleared away c.1570.

The church was patched up in 1633 for Charles I's coronation, when decorative reticulated tracery was introduced into the great east window, and the upper zone of the west front was embellished in a contemporary style. Over the

The west door of the Abbey Church.

LEFT: Inside the abbey. On the death of the Earl of Leven and Melville in 1906 it was announced that he had left £40,000 in his will to restore the Abbey Church so that it could once again serve as the Chapel of the Knights of the Thistle. After much debate it was decided that such an ambitious scheme would impair the archaeological integrity of the abbey ruins and the present Thistle Chapel was added to St Giles' Cathedral to the designs of Sir Robert Lorimer in 1909.

years the abbey has attracted many burials, including several Scottish kings and other members of the royal family. Such of their remains as could be rescued from the various phases of destruction are now interred in the Royal Vault in the ruins of the abbey, and surrounded by many handsome monuments.

In the nineteenth century the melancholy but picturesque ruins of the abbey were perfectly in tune with the presentation of the palace as the setting for much of the drama in the life of Mary, Queen of Scots, and it was a favourite subject for artists, especially when moonlight effects heightened the romantic atmosphere.

THE GARDENS AND ARTHUR'S SEAT

BELOW: The east front of Holyroodhouse, showing the gardens and the ruins of the abbey.

THE GARDEN OF THE PALACE cannot but be eclipsed by the sheer drama of the towering crags of Arthur's Seat, the core of an extinct volcano, which is encircled by the Queen's Park. This brings an extensive acreage of natural countryside into the very heart of the city. The gardens do not compete with so much natural beauty but rather through their air of well-tended cultivation form a contrasting foreground.

Like the Forecourt, the gardens suffered from over-zealous late Georgian and Victorian attempts to improve the palace's setting, but the resultant bleakness

This view of the ruins of the abbey, with hills rising in the background, gives an idea of the dramatic setting of the Palace of Holyroodhouse.

The gardens of the palace in 1913. The monument known as Queen Mary's sundial, carved by John Mylne in 1633, is visible before James V's Tower.

has been transformed by the luxuriant growth of screens of trees, introduced to hide the scars of industry such as breweries and gas-works, and the slum condition, by the nineteenth century, of many of the buildings at the lower end of the Royal Mile. The Prince Consort is said to have taken a particular interest in the schemes for the gardens, and perhaps the happiest and most ingenious feature of their design is the way in which the enclosing garden wall to the south-east replicates the effect of an original eighteenth-century ha-ha, or concealed ditch, and by thus concealing the actual boundary of the garden, gives the impression that it flows naturally into the park beyond.

In spite of this new breadth of vista, it is still to be regretted that the walled Privy Garden to the north of the Forecourt was so ruthlessly sacrificed for the new northern approach to the palace in 1856. Like so much else at Holyroodhouse, the Privy Garden was redolent of Mary, Queen of Scots. The two surviving relics are what was fancifully known as her sundial, but which was actually designed and carved by John Mylne in 1633, and the very much less securely dated and documented 'Queen Mary's bath', which may be a sixteenth-century garden building but whose precise history remains a mystery.